THE BEST TWEETS
FROM

ACTUARY

PROBLEM

DOG

Other books by the editor

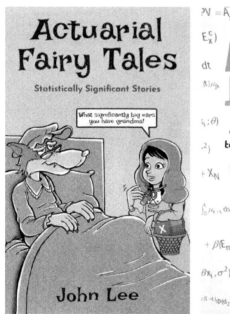

THE BEST TWEETS FROM

ACTUARY PROBLEM DOG

10 YEARS OF STATISTICALLY

INSIGNIFICANT HUMOR

Charities supported

A dollar/pound from every sale of this book will be given to the following charities, which work with those struggling with depression and other mental health issues:

Mental Health America (in USA)

MIND (in UK)

Acknowledgements

Actuary Dog would like to thank his fans who kept him tweeting, especially those who gave their permission to include their replies in this book.

The Dog would also like to thank Red Bull, Monster, coffee and McDonald's coke for helping keep him awake enough to squeeze more ~~tweets~~ study hours into the day.

The editor would like to thank the Dog for only needing a year of nagging before finally giving in and letting him create this book.

And the editor is extremely grateful to the following people who reviewed the original tweets to ensure only the very best remain: Akash Malpani, Adam Biros, Jessika Bossler, Greg Solomon, Kanishka Singhal, Karyn Cooke, Mary Pat Campbell and Nitin Raturi.

Glossary of American Terms

Since Actuary Problem Dog is American, some of his humor may not be immediately accessible to the rest of the world.

The editor therefore offers the following brief glossary, so that the full extent of the Dog's ~~depravity~~ wit can be enjoyed by all.

Actuarial terms

SOA   Society of Actuaries.
The largest American actuarial society that sets exams and professional standards for actuaries. It also seeks to absorb everything in its path.

CAS   Casualty Actuarial Society
Supports actuaries working in property & casualty insurance (called General Insurance in the UK).
Probably is a bit upset about the SOA's world domination.

ASA   Associate of the Society of Actuaries.
Someone who has passed the first 7 actuarial exams and is already half-way to losing their personality.

FSA   Fellow of the Society of Actuaries.
A fully qualified actuary. The journey to the dark side is now complete.

Exam P   One of the very first American actuarial exams, which tests probability and statistics via multi-choice.

Exam FM   Financial Mathematics.
Another of the very first American actuarial exams. It's also multi-choice, so it must be easy to pass.

MFE   Models for Financial Economics now renamed **IFM** (Investment & Financial Markets). Soon to be removed, much to the upset of all the actuaries who ever studied for it.

MLC	Models for Life Contingencies exam now called LTAM (Long-Term Actuarial Methods). Tests mathematics needed to model mortality used by life insurers and pensions. Soon to be called FAM as the actuarial exams are meant to take the place of any family you may have.
STAM	Short-Term Actuarial Mathematics exam which covers the statistical methods needed for modeling claims to a general insurer, *eg* motor. Soon to be called ALTAM or ASTAM, because having more letters makes it sound so much more menacing.
FAP	Fundamentals of Actuarial Practice An exam so named because the people at SOA didn't realize that FAP can mean something completely different...
APC	Associate Professionalism Course. The final requirement before becoming an Associate of the Society of Actuaries (ASA). Typically involves the removal of one's personality.
ERM	Enterprise Risk Management exam. An optional exam. Students who pass it get the letters CERA = Certificate in Enterprise Risk Management after their name. Four letters after your name might not seem much to non-actuaries, but it's a great substitute for personality.

Non-actuarial terms

Red Bull	A brand of energy drink. The advertising says that it "gives you wings" but statistical testing shows this to be false. Also, can anyone help clean up after my hypothesis test involving people drinking Red Bull and jumping off a roof produced more mess than expected under the drink's assumptions?
Monster	A brand of energy drink. Probably the name makes actuaries feel like they're doing something rebellious, when they're actually just studying or trying to meet a project deadline.
TI-30XS Multiview	A brand of calculator considered by Americans to be cool. Probably because they've never owned a Casio.

CONTENTS

SOCIAL INTERACTION 121

~~EAT~~ STUDY ~~SLEEP~~ (PART 2) 143

SOCIAL LIFE 169

THE END 181

INTRODUCTION

1st line of my book:

He's prone to be antisocial,

but he decided that if he didn't go to the

networking event he would kill himself, so he went.

The Story Behind Actuary Problem Dog

Why did you first start Actuary Problem Dog?

The mental stress of sitting the actuarial exams meant either I needed an *alter ego* or therapy to cope. And therapy was just too damn expensive.

Why Twitter and not Facebook?

As an actuary, I was naturally drawn to the small character limit. That my mom wasn't on there may have also had something to do with it, but correlation is not causation.

How did you come up with the name Actuary Problem Dog?

Because I love cats.

Why do you think Actuary Dog became so popular?

Actuaries are constantly looking to distract themselves from the gnawing emptiness that consumes them daily. And laughing at their empty lives is better than giving it up and becoming accountants.

IT'S AN ACTUARIAL LIFE

The girl at Starbucks acted like

she didn't even know that I'm an actuary!

What's an Actuary?

"No, I don't sell insurance - haven't had to make any cold calls except for the time I left my cell phone in the fridge."

Aw, you're a numbers guy!
You must do the family taxes & all that!

NAH ACCOUNTING IS BORING AF. I'M ONLY INTO HARDCORE SHIT LIKE JUDGMENT & MISERY.

Riddle me this Batman, what's an actuary?

Batman fails to save Gotham

Actuaries, in their own words

Whenever I try to explain what actuarial science is, it feels like someone took out a quarter of my brain and held me at gunpoint.

Actuary Problem Dog
@ActuaryDog

i look at all the numbers and summarize them into a few numbers then we meet and discuss certain numbers and execs decide on a final number

John Lee @Actuarial_Tutor
Replying to @ActuaryDog
Looks like your numbers up. #boomboomtish

Used to think being an actuarial science major was just a cool way to reveal that you need therapy. But there's so much more. So many dark holes.

My life is just one really bad improv show where the audience shouted 'study' as a suggestion.

Actuarial science, where taking a shower is a debtor's prison and the soap is dove guilt for men and the shampoo whispers, "why aren't you studying?"

Actuary Rules:

1) Pass exams

2) Keep a low profile

3) Make a nerdy comment every once & awhile

4) Don't recite digits from pi on the first date

Bro, you call yourself an actuary but don't even know the Gaussian probability density function lmaooo[1].

When actuaries die, we don't even update the mortality tables because actuaries are always on time and always behave as -E[X]pected-

---

[1] LMAO stands for Laugh My Ass Off. Probably part of Bayesian posterior analysis.

Why become an Actuary?

"Life too exciting?

Click here to learn how to be an actuary using this one really weird trick!" #studying

With all the wide scope of data sources available (big data), statisticians are now chefs... cooking up whatever conclusions are requested by the board.

puts on cape

"They must be stopped!"

 Actuary Problem Dog @ActuaryDog
Yes.

 jt @materium
Replying to @ActuaryDog
Wait so are these statisticians figurative criminals that figurative superhero actuaries have to stop?

Or are you saying actuaries have an obligation now to don a cooking apron to be the chef de cuisine who sends shit dishes back to the kitchen?

"50 PERCENT KNOWING WHAT I'M DOING COUPLED WITH 50 PERCENT MODERATELY CLUELESS MEANS EXCITING TIMES BEING AN ACTUARY."

If Actuaries Ruled the World

Is Actuarial Science a 'Cult'? (And Do Parents Care???) -CNN

We need an actuarial-themed restaurant "Ito's Lemma[2]-nade" "Taylor Series Infinite Breadsticks" "Meat Your Deductible - Meat lover's Pizza".

Hey you. Yes, you. You're on my Actuary Fantasy Team, so please pass your next exam and get those reports done on time.

Setting up a Microsoft Excel Only Fans[3] account. Wish me luck! Wish I could see the look on subscribers' faces when they accidentally become technically proficient in Excel as they look for other content!

---

[2] A complicated result used to derive option prices and derive actuarial students mad.

[3] An internet content subscription service that is used primarily by sex workers who produce content that doesn't typically involve spreadsheets.

Actuary Problem Dog
@ActuaryDog

happy to announce the new Actuary Dog meal at McDonald's starting October 1st!!!!
•iced red bull
•6-piece nugget (however you'll only get 5 if you are at least 90% but less than 100% of some random measure)
•three voicemails from recruiters asking if you want to "touch base"

Peter Yeates @peteryeates
Replying to @ActuaryDog
which sauce?

Actuary Problem Dog @ActuaryDog
sauce sparks too much joy. gotta stay focused peter!!!

So embarrassing! My Spotify Wrapped[4] Most Used Actuarial Formulas of 2020:

1. Simple addition

2. Simple subtraction

3. Actuarial judgment.

---

[4] Spotify is a music streaming provider, often used by actuaries to drown out the voice in their heads. Each year in December, Spotify wrapped allows its users to see their activity over the year.

"Tell me how you feel about that and please trend your feelings year-over-year with at least 30 specific examples." - actuarial psychologist

Actuary Problem Dog
@ActuaryDog

Actuarial Science, The Board Game
*rolls dice
you landed on... "drank 3 red bulls before bed then took ZQuil; wake up drowsy LOSE 1 FORMULA"

Anonymous
Replying to @ActuaryDog
One time I landed on "take NyQuil after last minute cramming, sleep through exam, LOSE A TURN".
I hate that game so much. [5]

---

[5] ZQuil = a brand of sleeping tablets. Nearly as effective as an actuarial meeting.

NyQuil = medicine used to help with cold, coughs, runny nose, and sleeplessness. True actuaries don't have time to get ill.

You might be an actuary if...

"Be right back. Gonna go grab the pizza."

Do you want me to pause the movie?

"No, I'm good. I'll just linearly interpolate between scenes."

The caffeine buzz at Starbucks is nice, but the numbers on the menu give me a stronger endorphin rush.

You know how people say we only use 10% of our brains? I think we only use 10% of our calculators.

Macklemore[6] has a song featuring Offset[7]...

More artists should feature Excel functions in their music!

I'm a little surprised Offset was picked over other functions, but I get the unique flavor it adds.

---

[6] American rapper and songwriter.

[7] Offset is the name of a rapper but is also used in Excel functions to allow formulas to dynamically adjust to inputs. Probably most actuaries had no idea of the rapper connotation.

Actuary Problem Dog
@ActuaryDog

well it looks like Cardi B and Offset are getting divorced

i know many of you have broken up with an excel function in your life as well (it was Vlookup for me)

sometimes it's for the best. dont get stuck in a dysfunctional relationship... even if it's with a function.

arj @RJaliciouss
Replying to @ActuaryDog
I left vlookup for index(match) and the whole neighborhood was gossiping about us 😏

  💬 2   🔁 1   ❤️ 4   ⬆️

Group Insurance Actuarial @ActuarialGroup
Replying to @RJaliciouss and @ActuaryDog
What if I am slowly losing affection for Excel and developing strong feelings for R?

When you turn 60, do you get a menu of chronic conditions to pick from or do they order for you?

We are all so lucky that there are multiple probabilistic decrements[8] competing for our death at all times.

---

[8] Ways of leaving a pension scheme, such as death, retirement or disability. These are also valid ways of escaping a trustee meeting.

Actuary Problem Dog
@ActuaryDog

you guys we have to change the name of prime numbers now that Amazon Prime is so popular in order to remain pure

Peter Yeates @peteryeates
Replying to @ActuaryDog
Wait ... you're saying the number on the label isn't a Prime Number?

When you hear someone say "projections" is it okay to get an adrenaline rush?

"If he treated a human being the way he treated that spreadsheet, he'd be in jail."

And to think this [COVID-19] all happened from one Excel simulation macro[9] breaking.

---

[9] A macro is a shortcut for undertaking multiple (often complicated) actions at once. To be honest, if you didn't know this then you most certainly aren't an actuary.

Geekdom (aka Cool Actuaries)

Actuaries do CrossFit every day by improperly lifting and dropping our 80 pound study manuals.

Actuary Problem Dog
@ActuaryDog

oh you got 3 monitors???

well i got 3 COMPUTERS bruh

and they're all on my desk and i keep using the wrong mouse and keyboard it's lit

Slope Software @SlopeSoftware
Replying to @ActuaryDog
look at you, all fancy and modern. here we are with our slide rules and aba... aba... abacu.... counting thingys.

Yeah, well, I have letters after my name too.

It's called my last name.

"I can't believe how many girls' numbers he got just by passing the P exam."

It's not a hickey[10] I slept on my calculat... err I mean yes it's a hickey!

"I sought out an all-knowing guru in India. He told me: in order to understand recursion, you must first understand recursion."

Actuary Problem Dog
@ActuaryDog

so many Happy Pi Day!!! mass texts today

7:04 PM · Mar 14*   11

---

[10] American word for a "love-bite" which is a bruise is formed by one person kissing or sucking the skin. This would require actuaries actually coming into close contact with another human being. I believe this last occurred in 1943.

[11] March 14 is abbreviated 3/14 in the American calendar and so is similar to 3.14, the first three values of pi. However, for everyone else in the world, March 14 is 14/3 which is not pi.

Things Actuaries Like

Not sure which is funnier/more true CPA [12] "can't pass actuarial" or FSA "formerly sexually active".

Actuary Problem Dog
@ActuaryDog

when the Actuary magazine comes in the mail

arj @RJaliciouss
Replying to @ActuaryDog
"6 different articles about talking to other humans effectively! Score!" [13]

---

[12] CPA = Certified Public Accountant. An inferior qualification.

[13] A monthly actuarial publication. Read by people who think watching paint dry is too exciting.

"No, I don't personally alter my lifestyle just because I can see the mortality tables." BUT SOMETIMES I BUY LOW CALORIE REDBULL.

Lawyers pass by a bar and be like 'I passed the bar.'

Actuaries pass by a bar and be like 'a-bar is actuarial notation for a continuous annuity.'

Regular ass people pass by a bar & have no thoughts because they're all simps[14].

Actuary Problem Dog
@ActuaryDog

yesss lets gooooo

Elon Musk @elonmusk · Jul 24, 2020
Replying to @Tesla
We are actually looking for revolutionary actuaries for Tesla Insurance! Please inquire, if interested.

John Lee @Actuarial_Tutor
Replying to @ActuaryDog
Wait - didn't you see it said "revolutionary".
I'm not sure using a pencil without sharpening it first counts.

---

[14] The originally meaning of simp was a man who is overly submissive to a woman that makes other guys cringe. Given that actuaries are unlikely to be in a relationship, let's just assume this context means someone who is just embarrassing to be around.

Me and other guys light up when we hear the word 'model' but not for the same reasons.

Laffy Taffy[15] rejected my riddles I don't get why

1. What do you call a large group of actuaries in Canada?

Answer: the S.O."eh"[16]

2. What do you call a new healthcare claim getting onto the highway?

Answer: "merging experience."

Happy New Year's Eve reminder not to drink & derive less you wanna end up in L'Hôpital[17].

---

[15] Laffy Taffy is an American brand of candy that has jokes printed on the outside of the wrapper. Presumably so people on a tight budget can laugh without having to spend money.

[16] Many Canadians add "eh" to the end of a sentence to express solidarity with the listener. Therefore S.O. "e"h sounds like SOA = Society of Actuaries. Missed opportunity for a CIA joke about the Canadian Institute of Actuaries.

[17] A mathematical rule used to find the value of 0 divided by 0. Kind of like an actuary dividing their social life by their number of friends.

ASOP[18] 23 & 41 walk into a bar.

ASOP 41 says I'll order the drinks clearly & concisely.

ASOP 23 says OK, I'll taste them both for reasonableness, but I won't audit the bartender's recipe.

Please register for my webinar "How to Achieve a Low-Stress Physical Appearance After Years of Social Anxiety, Exam PTSD, & Thousands of Excel Workbooks Saved on the Q:\ Drive That You'll Never Ever Open Again."

---

[18] ASOP = Actuarial Standards of Practice, which details how actuaries should carry out their work. ASOP 23 is on data quality; ASOP 41 is actuarial communications, which sadly doesn't give actuaries any advice on how to cope with small talk.

Actuary Problem Dog
@ActuaryDog

Walt Disney the Actuary: Lady sucks spaghetti at rate of μ and Tramp sucks spaghetti at rate of δ - what happens?

Actuaries and their children

Son, ask yourself what you want to be in the regression of life... a truly influential independent variable? Or a dummy variable?

"wtf dad?"

 Actuary Problem Dog
@ActuaryDog

daddy will you read me one of ASOPs fables before bed?
sure how about "The Tortoise and The Documentation of Data Quality"

 @saintphilip @saintphilip
Replying to @ActuaryDog
@ActuaryDog From the desk of ASOP's rival, ESOP: "The crow and the 'oh my god, you still fill these out with that typewriter!?'"

Reminder to consulting actuaries working from home with a child... keep track of their billable hours and send them an invoice once they're 18 years old.

Actuary Problem Dog @ActuaryDog
Federal Reserve announced new Inflation-Adjusted Math Flash Cards:
0x7 = 1
3x4 = 13
5x10 = 55
6x6 = 39
7x7 = 53
8x9 = 78

Actuary Problem Dog
@ActuaryDog

telling my kids this was the Kolmogorov–Smirnov test statistic

jt @materium
Replying to @ActuaryDog
Kids: "dad, do all actuaries have drinking problems?"

Actuary problem dog: "yes, and for once you don't need to hypothesis test this."

---

[19] The Kolmogorov-Smirnov test is used to see if data comes from a particular distribution. Smirnoff is a brand of vodka founded in Moscow by Pyotr Smirnov. I don't believe he used statistical distributions to make it, but I guess we'd need to carry out some kind of drinking hypothesis test to be sure.

Actuaries excel at Excel

airport security

"Sir, can you take out your laptop?"

Um, these Excel workbooks aren't mine!

"... what?"

I'll never use VLOOKUP again, I swear.

Actuary Problem Dog
@ActuaryDog

yep

I'm afraid that someday all of our abandoned Excel files will come to life and, like... make us feel bad.

 Actuary Problem Dog
@ActuaryDog

stop it

🔲 **Microsoft Excel** ✅ @msexcel · Jul 13, 2020
Anyone else had a chance to try out the new =CAKE function in Excel?
Show this thread

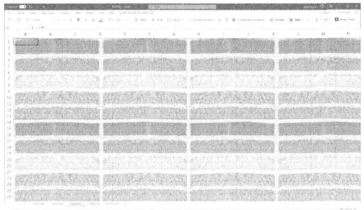

20

---

[20] Had this book been in color, you would have seen shades of red, orange, yellow, green and blue repeated. But since this book is for actuaries, I thought various shades of grey were more appropriate.

"My parents didn't talk to me about the dangers of having unprotected VLOOKUPS until I was like 20."

When the heck is Excel going to come out with a smart watch? I'm just lookin' for a quick 10×3 workbook I can wear on my wrist.

She said I'll be there for you - I laughed it off as a Friends reference, but she was serious... and that's when I told Excel that I love her.

Actuary Problem Dog
@ActuaryDog

when microsoft announced XLOOKUP...

21

---

[21] xlookup is a new Excel function that can replace both Index Match and vlookup. Actuaries are hopeful that it can also replace the need for meaningful relationships.

The Dark Side of the Actuarial Moon

Only reason I haven't killed myself is because they'd just make me the analytics guy in hell and I can't even imagine how bad their data is.

When bae[22] scrolls through your calculator history and sees that you punched in 100*1.05. ☹

If you're an actuary whatever you do, DON'T GET A TOUCH SCREEN LAPTOP!

You literally touch the data in Excel, and like drag it, and like feel it that physical relationship may evolve into something more serious and you will no longer be able to remain objective and independent!

---

[22] Bae stands for "Before Anyone Else" and is used as an affectionate term to refer to one's girlfriend, boyfriend or spouse. Since actuaries are unlikely to be in a relationship, they typically use this term to refer to Excel or their calculator.

Actuary Problem Dog
@ActuaryDog

how come at the 2016 Olympics in Rio they handed out a record 450,000 condoms but at actuarial seminars they hand out 0 condoms

stuart mcdonald @ActuaryByDay
Replying to @ActuaryDog
Because the world needs more actuarial babies!

Betsy Craig @EECraig
Replying to @ActuaryDog
Because supply meets demand.

"When I was your age, I had to learn math from graffiti sprayed on the trains in Chicago."

My second worst fear is having to make friends based on my personality traits.

It's not anxiety, it's stress testing

Actuary Problem Dog
@ActuaryDog

how can i simply wake up and eat breakfast when there's so much i don't know that i don't know

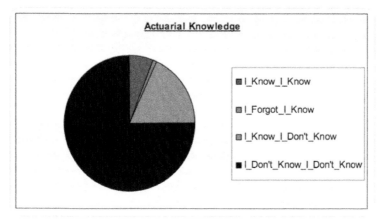

My worst fear is that nothing bad ever happens to me.

I'm so competitive I need to have more anxiety than everyone else.

It's not OCD, it's attention to detail

If you even so much as think about using 22/7 as a quick substitute for π I'm not sure we can be friends.

"Can't believe he needed a grocery list to buy Pepsi and M&M's."

Might be "socially unacceptable" to call you at 4am but I'm solving a system of equations in my head & need you to know I can be spontaneous.

Too much pressure to find the absolute best deal, therefore I'm never ordering pizza ever again.

EAT STUDY ~~SLEEP~~ (PART 1)

I want me one of those ASA things

Actuarial Exams

We will create a series of professional level math-based exams, they said. Candidates will fill the emptiness in their hearts, they said.

Why are actuarial exams so difficult?

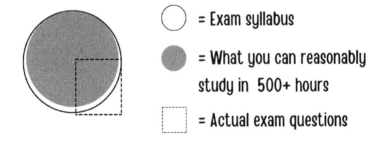

◯ = Exam syllabus

⬤ = What you can reasonably study in 500+ hours

▢ = Actual exam questions

"Exam P is supposed to weed you out, but some people actually study for it."

"That guy on the motorcycle probably cut me off because he knows I don't have my ASA yet."

"MFE? Is that the exam where you need to know Brownian motion?"

Yes, it's also the one where you need long-term psychological rehabilitation.

Life may be defined as BE and AE, before and after exams.

My study manual has just as many pages as the Bible.

The novelty of becoming an actuary wears off like 4 exams in.

Final draft of study terminology I'm sending to the SOA:

Study Session = 1-2 hrs

"Wired-in" = 3-4 hrs

Study Rager = 5-6 hrs

Bender = 7+ hrs.

Once I get my ASA...

"Once I get my ASA, everyone on the street will know who I am and want to take pictures with me."

When I get my ASA, I'm putting those letters on everything.
"I'll have a Grande pumpkin spice latte, please.
The name is Actuary Dog, ASA."

Can't wait to get my ASA so I can take a week off from studying.

Ongoing list of things to do after exams:

- find a hobby

- work harder

- give my cat a hickey

- visit more than 3 websites

- get mental help.

Tips & Tools of the Trade

You are given a $15 budget to pass your actuarial exam. How are you building your life?

Price	Social Life	Study Time	Study Materials	Diet	Work-Life Balance
$5	Significant Other	500 Hours	Source Material + In-Person Seminar + Notecards + Practice Problems + Study Guide	Tenderloin steaks, eggs, avocado toast, coffee	40-hours stress free work, Exercise 5x week, Sleep 8-9 hrs/night
$4	Pets	400 Hours	In-Person Seminar + Notecards + Practice Problems + Study Guide	Chipotle, diet soda	45-hours work, Exercise 3x week, Sleep 7-8 hrs/night
$3	Friends in Person	300 Hours	Notecards + Practice Problems + Study Guide	Jimmy Johns, energy drinks	50-hours stressful work, Exercise 2x week, Sleep 7 hrs/night
$2	Friends Virtually (FB, Insta, Snapchat)	200 Hours	Practice Problems + Study Guide	Wendy's & sugar-free red bull	60-hours stressful work, Exercise 1x week, Sleep 6 hrs/night
$1	Strangers online (Twitter)	100 Hours	Study Guide & I'll look at some old exam problems	Ramen, tuna packets, & whatever's in the fridge	I'm a Consultant

I named my study manual "Furby[23]" because it annoys me and makes me feel guilty when I don't give it attention (it's also cute).

Study tip: try altitude training by doing practice exams on a cold mountain.

---

[23] A Furby was an annoying electronic talking pet that looked like a cross between an owl and a hamster. Easy to confuse with actuarial summer interns.

Actuary Problem Dog
@ActuaryDog

you have to be ready for anything on exam day
will the desk be SMOOTH? will it be ONLY KIND OF
SMOOTH?
will life still be MEANINGFUL?

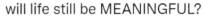

Avraham Adler @AvrahamAdler
Replying to @ActuaryDog
two calculators
extra batteries
eyeglass scredriver to open back
three mechanical pencils
two containers of lead
one full-length eraser.

Study tip for MLC mortality problems: prepare for them like it's a matter of life or death.

It's ~~Hammer~~ Study Time

Hey man, thanks for the $ here's your study manual. Wanna stick around and take a hit off this MFE problem with me? It's some premium stuff!

Throw a bunch of practice problems in a room full of actuarial students and watch them go! #puppybowl

"I was going to do a few more problems before bed, but I didn't want to trigger an endorphin rush."

I'm worried that my memory foam pillow will become so adaptive that it will pass all of the exams faster than me.

"Hi mom, let me call you later. I'm about to do a triathlon."

*reads source material

*reviews flash cards

*works practice problems

This one goes out goes to all my ladies doing practice problems without formula sheets nearby & my fellas who use Excel in their spare time.

Beer Pong[24], except each cup has a practice problem inside and you don't actually have any friends.

My physical therapist said it's helpful to cross-train so I'm gonna take the Certified Public Accountant (CPA) exam.

---

[24] A drinking game in which players throw a ping pong ball across the table trying to get it in a cup of beer on the other end. If successful, the opponent has to drink said cup of beer. The British version involves throwing biscuits in cups of tea.

Actuary Problem Dog
@ActuaryDog

they haven't asked an exam question on cumulative antiselection theory in over 10 years

OK I'LL ONLY SPEND 5 FULL DAYS ON THAT

John Lee @Actuarial_Tutor
Replying to @ActuaryDog
Aha - thinking the examiner is a malevolent opponent and so focusing on the worst case scenario. Good work.

"He's such a lightweight - it only takes him 6 practice problems to get a study buzz going."

I've studied just enough today to develop an interest in what my coworkers' weekend plans are.

Dang! I think I left my study manual in the oven while I was making the pizza. Oh well.

Things in life were a lot simpler when all I had to think about was 8×8=64. Now 8×8=64 is more of a nostalgic vibe.

Procrastination vs Guilt – who will win?

I'm counting the time I spent on Actuarial Outpost[25] as study hours.

"I can't wait to go home so I can open up all my study materials and then just sit there and stare at the wall."

Thanks Daylight Savings now I have to procrastinate an extra hour tonight.

"I'll have to set aside at least 5 hours if I'm going to study for 2 hours, so I might as well try studying tomorrow instead."

---

[25] ActuarialOutpost.com was a discussion forum that was *the* place for American actuaries to hang out. Until the new owners decided to delete all the funny posts and make it more serious. Now GoActuary.com is *the* new place to hang out, or Reddit or any other dark corners of the internet that actuaries can congregate without accountants mocking them.

The SOA is google mapping you right now and knows that you're not studying.

Actuary Problem Dog
@ActuaryDog

when you're out having a good time but then you remember your exam is in less than 2 months

Pressure & perseverance

These exams are only offered twice a year, no pressure though!

I just got up to go to the bathroom started thinking about how much studying I have to do tonight and I forgot to go to the bathroom.

People often ask, "How do you know when you're ready for the exam?" When you look at yourself in the mirror and your reflection doesn't look back.

Actuary Problem Dog
@ActuaryDog

guess what season is CHAMPIONSHIP EXAM SEASON

spring	6.6%
summer dread	9.8%
FALL GLOOM GRIT AND GRIND	59%
suicidal winter	24.6%

61 votes · Final results

I'm either going to study tonight or have an existential meltdown. I can't decide.

"I want my coffin to be a giant sized, fully functioning TI-30 XS Multiview."

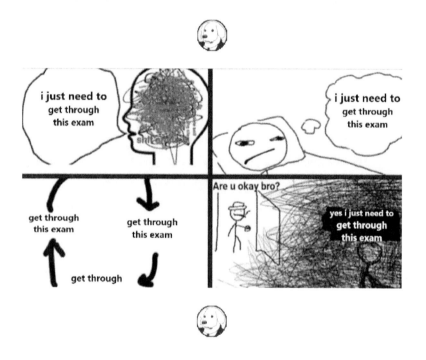

You can study 130 hours a week, if you plan your showers appropriately.

If you don't dream about doing problems and wake up shouting equations, then I'm sorry but you're not ready to take the exam.

My worst fear is that I don't wake up with the same anxiety and stresses I worked so hard for today.

I only studied 3 hours today. Tomorrow my plan is to roofie[26] myself with Red Bull and crank out a marathon 10-hour study rager.

But can the reinsurers also reassure me that everything will be okay?

---

[26] Drug assault, not someone who fixes roofs.

Going on a 16-hour bender at the office tomorrow; live tweets starting at 7:30am. #OfficeRager #Excel #cubicle #carpaltunnel #staledonut

Hour 9 of 16: it's getting dark at the office - thinking about my cat all alone at home, but then who will take care of my Excel if I leave?

Hour 12 of 16: all lights turned off except for my dimly lit PC monitor -a symbol for how actuaries are completely in the dark without Excel.

The exam

I thought studying was dark and depressing but it affects people differently. Like this one guy literally brought a cooler into the exam room and acted like it gave him an advantage that he could drink multiple Snapples[27] and not piss his pants (he failed).

"I'll just learn the problems I don't know while I'm taking the exam."

Starting Lineup announced for exam day:

Calculator: TI-30XS Multiview

Pen: black uni-ball Signo-RT 0.7mm

Pencil: BIC mechanical HB #2 0.7mm.

---

[27] Fruit flavored drinks. Not typically known for their enhanced actuarial thinking properties.

Actuary Problem Dog
@ActuaryDog

"he's gotten so good at taking exams that he can take them with almost any type of pencil"

John Lee @Actuarial_Tutor
Replying to @ActuaryDog
@ActuaryDog He'll be in trouble taking the UK exams as it requires use of a black pen...

Cramming for an actuarial exam is like listening to a band's CD for the first time on the way to the concert.

Actuary Problem Dog
@ActuaryDog

YOUR EXAM CHANCES
Single No Pets No Friends 66%
Single w/ Pets or Friends 40%
SigOther No Pets No Friends 33%
SigOther w/Pets or Friends 25%

Kimbaaaaaaly @HeyKimmerz
Replying to @ActuaryDog
married with kids, 0%.

John Lee @Actuarial_Tutor
Replying to @tweetsbyIanB and @ActuaryDog
I started the exams with one & finished with 4. Clearly I found something to do to relieve the boredom of revision

The results

If you have Amazon Prime, you should get your SOA results faster.

Today we find out if a day we had 80 days ago was a good day or not.

(exam results day)

(dread, existential)

Happy exam results day to 40% of you!!!

Actuarial student - lives for the euphoric release of an exam pass only to be celebrated with another 500-hour grind for the next one.

Actuary - lives for back-to-back 60-hour weeks to produce a report good enough to get that euphoric "OK, sounds good thanks" from your boss.

"Stop crying. It's just a movie!"

The movie:

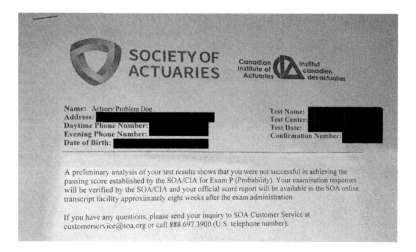

"Life goes on" -the darkest attempt to feel better after a failed exam.

Give me a calculator to cry on...

Exam passer loses it all by spending $2,500 exam raise on $1.6 million house in Palm Beach Gardens.

Actuary Problem Dog
@ActuaryDog

exam celebration begins   !!!!

The after math

You can tell she has all her exams passed because there's a glowing aura around her (abstract personality & low stress physical appearance).

Ghost of Exams Past was so mean to me this year. Woke me up in the middle of the night to be like, "Remember when u studied on Christmas Eve while your dad had to install windows 8 all by himself?"

Every time I see the Gamma symbol, my eyes glaze over like Bambi.

I forced a bot to take over 10,000 hours of SOA exams and then asked it to write an exam of its own. Here is the first question:

BEGINNING OF EXAMINATION

1. (*666 points*) In 2022, you work for Heads Falling Off Insurance Company as an internal consultant in a post-apocalyptic society. Your company's artificial intelligence medical doctors were so efficient in curing diseases that they eventually saw human life as a disease and exterminated most of the human race. You will soon be faced with the life penalty for failing to include "human extermination" as an assumption in your Enterprise Risk Model. If you are given the life penalty, you will never be able to feel the sweet release of death.

    Humans follow a multi-state transition model as follows:

    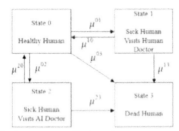

    You are given the following constant transition intensities:

    (i) $\mu^{01} = 0.004$
    (ii) $\mu^{10} = 0.006$
    (iii) $\mu^{02} = 0.005$
    (iv) $\mu^{03} = 0.002$
    (v) $\mu^{23} = 0.001$
    (vi) $p^{33} = 1.000$

    (a)   (*666 points*) Calculate the probability of human extinction within the next 5 years.

    Your models were reviewed by Amazon's army of AI drone actuaries and it was determined that your pre-apocalypse assumptions were grossly insufficient.

    You were charged with "unreasonable actuarial assumptions" and are sentenced to immortal life on Earth.

    Your soul will be collected by an Amazon drone within 3-5 business days.

I'd have to ask my mom, but I'm pretty sure the exams took parts of my soul. I view humanity as just a math problem now.

Never blacked out from alcohol, but I might have since I memorized so many formulas that I can't remember anything that happened between 2011-2014.

RELATIONSHIPS

Is love statistically significant?

Starting out

"I'd have a girlfriend if I could put it on my resume."

If you're single, celebrate!

Today could be your negative-3-year anniversary with someone you haven't even met yet!!!!!

How am I supposed to explain to her what actuarial science is if OkCupid[28] only has a 10,000 character limit?

Someone please audit the following text to a girl:

"Hey there! How's your week going, writing lots of Excel macros?????[29]"

---

[28] OkCupid is a dating website. However, it's only fair of me to tell you that, as an actuary, your chances of finding a match there are still slim to nothing.

[29] Personally, I think one more question mark ought to do it.

When a girl endorses a guy on LinkedIn for "Excel", does that mean she wants him to ask her out on a date?

"Go for it, bro! Maybe she has a nerd fetish and won't think it's weird that you talk to your calculator."

Pickup lines

"So, how do you like sitting next to the printer?"

-office pickup lines.

"I know three other languages," was a great bar pickup line until he said "... SQL, SAS, and VBA[30]."

"Hey girl, Excel may be limited to 1,048,376 rows but my heart is like a whole folder of Excel workbooks just for you."

Actuary Problem Dog
@ActuaryDog

can i see your p-values

Jon Sharp @Pension_Jon
Replying to @ActuaryDog
For an appropriate fee and after a proportionate peer review ...[31]

---

[30] Types of computer languages used for data bases, statistical analysis and Excel, respectively. Typically actuaries speak these more fluently than their own language.

[31] A p-value is a measure of the probability of rejecting a true hypothesis. Not to be confused with the volume of urine passed after an evening on the town.

actuary trying to pick up girl at a wedding ice cream bar

"I noticed you anti-select against the leaner coverage[32], opting for low fat vanilla."

Actuary Problem Dog
@ActuaryDog

hey girl wanna come over and see my multiviews?

"omg you have a balcony with multiple views? we can watch the sunset!"

yeah when you press down on the screen it makes really pretty colors!!!

jt @materium
· Replying to @ActuaryDog
Hey girl, I professionally model.

Let me just open up Excel.

Hey babe, wanna get drunk and watch previously recorded SOA webinars?

---

[32] Anti-selection (also known as adverse selection) is where one side in an insurance contract uses extra information to gain an advantage over the other. Also used by actuaries against accountants.

How we met?

How'd you guys meet, L-O-V-LOOKUP?

Nah man, we found each other on INDEX-MATCH.COM[33]. The relationship doesn't break when you add a column.

"I opened an Excel workbook that she was already working in. It was like we held hands and kissed."

"How'd you meet?"

We met on an app called Microsoft Excel. I opened a file she was already in. But our relationship is no longer 'Read-Only'.

---

[33] VLOOKUP and INDEX-MATCH are Excel functions that allow you to look up values from a table. However, INDEX-MATCH is considered superior. Possibly because it has the letter X in its name.

First Date

First date: "what are the top risks that terrify you?"

- blank stare risk

- failing an exam risk

- small talk risk

- first day of work no pants

I'm hoping that the tiny bit of charm I have divided by my awkwardness will still be enough for her to like me.

"I just want someone who will love me for my body and not for my mind."

Take a shot c'mon take a shot c'mon it's New Year's Eve, just take a shot!

girl takes shot at MFE problem, falls in love with actuarial science

Maybe that girl didn't make out with me last night because she thought I only had one exam...

What Actuaries Like

You had me at "Golden Ratio[34]."

I'm not a sexual person, but for some reason nothing turns me on more than seeing numbers neatly organized in a table with column headings.

She made an active listening sound during my presentation (and it felt like a kiss).

"... but most of all, I love the way she rolls up claims data - it's so beautiful."

---

[34] The Golden Ratio is a special number approximately equal to 1.618 that appears many times in mathematics, geometry, art, architecture and other areas. However, it doesn't appear much in conversation with non-geeks.

She's a 5 but with Bath n Body works sensual amber perfume, she's easily a 7 and actuaries know anything higher than 6 passes[35].

IF YOU SLEEP WITH YOUR STUDY MANUAL, THEN I LOVE YOU.

"You look like a tired actuary on their fourth Red Bull." <-- hottest thing you can say to someone.

---

[35] The American actuarial exams give students a score from 0 to 10, where 6 or higher represents a pass. 5 represents a student who will tell everyone how they *nearly* passed it if only it hadn't been for *insert excuse here*.

Actuarial Dating Tips

Dating tip: girls know it's not about how big your sample size is, it's how you use it.

With just a few shock therapy treatments & some discipline, you can actually train yourself to not bring up exams every time you go on a date.

Dating tip: don't ask her what she thinks about the ACA[36] until at least after they put the bread and butter out.

Like MLC, texting girls should include a 15 minute read-through time and 3 hours to solve.

Apparently, girls don't really care how many digits you can recite from the number pi.

---

[36] ACA = Affordable Care Act (aka Obamacare). A massive shake-up in health insurance which meant that people with pre-existing conditions had to be covered for those conditions. Necessarily this led to a massive rise in premiums.

St Valentine's Day

It's Valentine's Day so I'm reflecting on the closest connection I've ever felt to someone... going through a study manual front to back & doing every single practice problem. It's like you know the author can feel your heart beating faster with each correct answer.

"Babe, no one else meets my minimum requirements like you. Happy Valentine's Day."

Babe, I'm going to die someday. You're going to die someday, but we're both here right now... so let's spend years of our lives taking exams.

Roses are red

Association health plans are cheap,

But they don't cover much

So have fun giving birth in your jeep.

Actuary Problem Dog
@ActuaryDog

happy valentine's day to that one special Linkedin person, masked behind a paywall

		LinkedIn	Social	**You appeared in 1 search this week**	- You appeared in 1 search
		LinkedIn	Social	**You appeared in 1 search this week**	- You appeared in 1 search
		LinkedIn	Social	**You appeared in 1 search this week**	- You appeared in 1 search
		LinkedIn	Social	**1 person is noticing you**	- See who's looking at your profile
		LinkedIn	Social	**1 person is noticing you**	- See who's looking at your profile
		LinkedIn	Social	**You appeared in 1 search this week**	- You appeared in 1 search
		LinkedIn	Social	**1 person is noticing you**	- See who's looking at your profile
		LinkedIn	Social	**1 person is noticing you**	- See who's looking at your profile
		LinkedIn	Social	**1 person is noticing you**	- See who's looking at your profile
		LinkedIn	Social	**1 person is noticing you**	- See who's looking at your profile
		LinkedIn	Social	**1 person is noticing you**	- See who's looking at your profile
		LinkedIn	Social	**1 person is noticing you**	- See who's looking at your profile
		LinkedIn	Social	**1 person is noticing you**	- See who's looking at your profile
		LinkedIn	Social	**1 person is noticing you**	- See who's looking at your profile
		LinkedIn	Social	**1 person is noticing you**	- See who's looking at your profile

Developing your relationship

If you meet a girl at a bar, how long do you have to wait before you endorse her for VBA macros on LinkedIn?

You don't really know someone until you see the inside of their Excel workbooks.

Expressing Actuarial Emotion

Babe, my feelings for you are... *pulls C exam formula sheets out of pocket* ... um lognormally distributed

Girls like you only come around once in a lifetime -not that I think a lifetime is statistically significant - but still, babe, you're special.

"If I had billable hours and had to bill all of my thoughts to a client, I would bill them all to you, babe. I love you."

I love staring into your beautiful spreadsheet eyes, babe THOSE COLUMNS THOSE ROWS.

kisses wife goodnight

"You're the only one I would stop solving a system of equations to be with."

Babe, my love for you is recursive, but in order to understand recursion, you must first understand recursion.

"Good night babe, add another day to our decline."

Decline?

"Our declining longevity," *kisses cheek*

Longevity?

"You know what, babe? Never mind."

Engagement & Marriage

"We need to have at least 18 months of historical data before we get engaged."

Babe, wait! I'm saving that free month of LinkedIn premium for our honeymoon.

"I would memorize any formula for you," as a wedding vow.

I vow to always treat you like the source material and never summarize or water down your personality for my own short-term convenience based on someone else's perception.

Marriage is like auto-renewing an annual policy based on just a few years' good experience and only like 40% credibility

The two loves: Work vs Women

"Stop babe, I'm trying to study the time value of money."

"Well, maybe you should study the time value of HONEY... you know... ME?"

"Wish I didn't."

"I'd rather be sick on my wedding day than miss an hour of work."

I take my wedding ring off when I study because I don't want my exam materials to question my commitment to lifelong learning.

You guys, I'm goin' off the rails. I just called my wife by my ex-company's name: I love you too UNITED HEALTH, it just slipped out!

making out

Oh yes SUMIF I love you, yes yes!

intensifies

My sweet MACRO

kisses neck

You are my ABSOLUTE ROW and COLUMN you filthy VLOOKUP

(kissing stops)

"... umm I'm really sorry but I'd prefer if you used INDEX-MATCH[37]."

---

[37] Names of various functions in Excel. INDEX-MATCH is considered superior to VLOOKUP. You could say that actuaries look down on VLOOKUP...

Actuarial Intimacy

Statistically, making out requires the highest amount of work for the least amount of bragging rights.

Baby, kiss me like you just passed an exam.

"... What?"

And maybe whisper a formula in my ear - nothing cheesy tho' no Pythagorean Theorem shit.

@cosmopolitan Can talking about risk adjustment and Itô's lemma be considered foreplay? Thanks in advance!

Babe, sorry, the only sex move I know is when the demographics shift in such a way that the M-F ratio goes from 51%-49% to 49%-51%. Is that hot?

"I can't make love unless there are spreadsheet sheets on the bedsheets."

Actuary Problem Dog
@ActuaryDog

half hour of foreplay when literally this would turn you on
$100 * 1.07 = $107

marfle @eirsalazar
Replying to @ActuaryDog
but written as force of interest makes it feel so much more spontaneous

The first time I had sex I didn't like it because I had nothing to compare it to so I used a weighted average of a swimming pool and a jet ski.

After you pass one exam, you have to go cliff jumping just to keep your sex drive going.

Risk Management

"Hey girl, is it okay if I cc my friend Robbie on all our texts so I can get advice on how to respond?"

Guys, what's more politically correct: "she could lose a few pounds," or "she resembles a Burr distribution (heavy-tailed)"?

Actuary Problem Dog
@ActuaryDog

why do i always have to MATHSPLAIN things to my wife

stuart mcdonald @ActuaryByDay
Replying to @ActuaryDog
You didn't marry another actuary? I didn't realise actuaries were allowed to pair off with normals?

A DAY IN THE LIFE OF AN ACTUARY

I'm not afraid of being wrong,
I'm afraid of being right and having no idea why.

Interns

Actuary Problem Dog
@ActuaryDog

fav thing about new interns?

hope in their voices	19%
false epiphanies	12.4%
eyes blink like bambi	20%
they still have a soul	48.6%

Actuary intern walks into a doctor's office

"What's wrong?"

I have a big presentation tomorrow & I just feel awful. I'm nauseous & have a sharp pain in my abdomen.

"I'm afraid we're going to have to remove your appendix."

We can maybe take out Appendix C, but what about the pain?

Intern: "boss you need anything?"

Yeah, can you read my mind & then type up the report?

intern finally learns what it means to be an actuary

Actuary Problem Dog
@ActuaryDog

my favorite thing about actuarial interns is we'd be at churchill downs you'd hear their INSANELY LOUD celebrations and excitement only to find out they bet $5 on the 2-1 favorite to finish top 3 in a 6-horse race & won like 15 cents

Catuary @Catuary1
Replying to @ActuaryDog
As an intern who worked remotely this summer I just want to say, wait we were suppose to interact with each other?

John Lee @Actuarial_Tutor
Replying to @Catuary1 and @ActuaryDog
I concur - sounds like they're not cut out to be proper actuaries...

Slope Software @SlopeSoftware
Replying to @ActuaryDog
hey, fifteen cents is fifteen cents.

38

---

[38] Churchill Downs is a horse racetrack. Why the actuaries were out in public is the most worrying thing about this whole scenario.

Interview

Interview Tip: A few days before the interview, break into the office to see what it looks like. This will help you get mentally prepared.

Should I list my top 3 calculators on my resume or just wait for the on-site interview?

LIST IT AND MAKE SURE YOU HAVE BA II PLUS[39].

Interview tip: just start talking and hope that your problem-solving skills will kick in and get you to the right answer.

Interview tip: just end every answer with "and it was a great experience!"

---

[39] A financial calculator with a hefty price tag. But what else are actuaries going to spend money on, given that they don't have any social life?

I've no idea what I'm doing

Half my job is being given something no one understands and being asked to explain it to management.

I said "yeah that makes sense" so many times at work today and now I'm afraid to ask questions and nothing makes sense.

Work Acronyms Explained, Pt. IV

EOD = End of Day (report is due at midnight)

EOB = End of Bae[40] (she's gone) (forever) (she's not coming back)

"Sometimes if you just sit there and stare at a spreadsheet long enough, it actually does start to make sense."

---

[40] Bae stands for "Before Anyone Else" – kind of like "My other half". Don't worry, as an actuary, there's plenty of study and work deadlines to fill the other half.

If I ask a question in the meeting, it may reveal that I don't know something, but if I don't ask, it reveals that I don't know what I don't know.

"No boss, I have no idea who accidentally printed out 900 pages of SAS[41] code and then spent the morning hiding under their desk who was that."

"Ooooohhhhh, so that's what my manager explained to me at my desk 3 months ago."

---

[41] SAS = a computer package used by statisticians to analyze data. Not to be confused with British special forces.

Emails

"I only sent one email today, but it was like super actuarial."

Who's that guy always CCd on emails but never says anything? Must be important!

If you're going to send me a screenshot of an Excel workbook, then I don't know why I'm even here.

Took me 3 hours to write a 2 sentence email, because they pay me to over-analyze not to write emails.

Actuary Problem Dog
@ActuaryDog

"Please stop replying all to this email chain"
"Hello - am I supposed to get this?"
"Please stop sending emails"
"Please remove me off these emails as they are not applicable to me and my role"
"Any way you can stop sending these?"
"What is this and why are they coming??????????"

Actuary Problem Dog @ActuaryDog
Replying to @ActuaryDog
we had a reply-all chain that lasted 47 responses today before it finally stopped

as i read each response, i laughed, cried, and related on a deeply spiritual level with so many people who simply do not want to be bothered

Boss, I'm not saying you need to reply back right away.

I'm just saying that most of my emails are written by someone in character who thinks he is about to die and needs your answer to live.

Modeling

I JUST WANT THE RAW DATA, MAYBE MEDIUM RARE EVEN IF I HAVE TO ANALYZE EACH CLAIM ONE BY ONE AS IT COMES IN I DON'T EVEN CARE.

Actuary Problem Dog
@ActuaryDog

i love when you get a dataset and it's named something like
"SEVERITY_SCORE_TABLE_TEMP6"

it's like "guys time is fleeting we are all temporary even this data"

we are nothing more than a TEMPv6 slowly drifting into the void

mlschop @mlschop
Replying to @ActuaryDog
My favorite is when I get a file sent to me with a name like "ABC final v3 final final.xls"

It's sad because it's definitely happened more than once...

Boss, we should probably just throw out all the data since our planet is a huge outlier in the solar system.

None of these patterns matter! The data is just going to restate next quarter. Nothing matters! Life is just a restatement of a restatement.

Actuary Problem Dog
@ActuaryDog

i promise my projections for next year will be more accurate

🐶 **Actuary Problem Dog** @ActuaryDog
new 2016 trendspotting:
mint-flavored craft hamburgers
fitbits for animals
microwaveable nba jerseys
keyboard tattoos that work with iPads

Predictions for the rest of 2021:

- stock market crash in April

- Betty White dies (sorry Betty)

- my wife never eats the banana chips she bought.[42]

---

[42] Score: 2 out of 3. RIP Betty.

Actuary Problem Dog
@ActuaryDog

we once had a morbidity regression that took over 8 hours to process in SAS and would always break towards the end

my entire 2017 thanksgiving break was spent trying to fix it

looks like they finally made a movie based on it

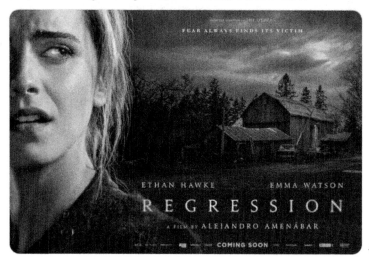

43

Payroll and jobs report was good. It was only life expectancy that dropped, thank God.

---

43 SAS = a computer package used by statisticians to analyze data. A morbidity regression model predicts the probabilities of people getting ill. It probably notices a mysteriously high correlation between illness and Mondays.

Presenting results

Hey boss, here's my projection based on 1% of data. Let's schedule a call and discuss in exhausting detail.

Every monthly presentation is an audition for your own job-no pressure, though!

My boss accepted my meeting 'Tentatively.' Maybe he's commenting on the futility of life and showing disdain for assumed future certainties.

Meeting to talk about the upcoming meeting followed by the actual meeting and a meeting to discuss meeting takeaways PLEASE SEND HELP.

"Hope my presentation gets a better reaction than it did when I practiced for my stuffed animals."

I tried giving a presentation "actuarial webinar style" where you literally read a pre-made script of everything you are going to say and GUYS I WOULD NOT RECOMMEND IT.

It ended up sounding like I was reading a pre-made script.

Literally nothing more satisfying than putting together an extremely thorough analysis, presenting it to your boss, and getting that euphoric "OK sounds good, thanks."

My favorite question to get from leadership is... why are these two different forecasts, based on different populations and different assumptions, built up at different granularities... giving us DIFFERENT RESULTS?

CEO: explain the model to me like you would to a 5-year-old.

OK, no problem... it's a supervised learning algorithm using repeated partitioning of the explanatory variables to form homogeneous groups that ultimately predict when your mommy and daddy are going to die!

Deadlines

Friday

That Monday headache is finally gone, time to do some work!!

"You don't have to stay late and do it today, but the client needs this by tomorrow and I'm leaving now and it takes a few hours to do."

Actuary Problem Dog
@ActuaryDog

"omggg we're not gonna get the report out in time!!!"

wait, i have an idea... let's call the client and ask if they've set their clocks back yet!!

"by george we might just pull this off!!!!!!!"

Peter Yeates @peteryeates
Replying to @ActuaryDog
Timezone arbitrage is alive and kicking

"Can I go home, boss? I already had my 40 hours at noon on Wednesday."

The need for coffee

Sometimes I drink decaf just for the placebo effect.

NOT TODAY THO' BOSS I'M ALL IN.

Testing my hypothesis that it's better to be tired but on two large Dunkin' Donuts iced coffees than well-rested without any caffeine.

"There's a fine line between caffeine-drinking productivity techniques and turning into a horny rage filled, vindictive werewolf."

Actuary Problem Dog
@ActuaryDog

coffee hangovers aren't that bad i just get 15 second blackouts every now and then

Peter Yeates @peteryeates
Replying to @ActuaryDog
Need to confirm they're independent and identically distributed

The dedication

When I first started, all of the new hires had breakfast with the chief actuary.

I was so nervous, over-analyzing everything and thought so carefully about my body language and vibe.

Then someone asked him if he ever had oatmeal from McDonald's and something inside me died.

Just cracked open a can of green Monster "better update the mortality tables".

It's almost like we're just trading large amounts of self-inflicted pain just for a mildly approving head nod from our boss.

Boss, I didn't see you online yesterday.

"It was a company holiday."

Hmm, must be nice to follow societal constructs and define yourself by time.

Happy Halloween boss! I painted you a pumpkin with the corporate logo using my blood.

"Boss, my Excel keeps freezing because I'm trying to be more efficient by having 26 windows open."

For this year's performance review, we are just going to look to see if you have bloodshot eyes and broken dreams. If so, then you can stay.

Can you get fired for recording everything your coworkers say on a tape recorder and then studying it?

You guys, there are people behind these numbers don't say "risk factor of 1.4".

Say it with respect

"risk factor"

sign of the cross

"of 1.4."

"Maybe my boss doesn't call me to hang out on weekends because he secretly looks down on me for not having LinkedIn premium."

I don't need serotonin or weekends because I'M SO AFRAID OF BEING AN ACTUAL FUNCTIONING PERSON WAIT HANG ON IS THERE ANY PIZZA LEFT.

"If he's working during the Super Bowl, it must mean he's inefficient & can't manage his time OR we are understaffed and there's too much to do."

Actuarial Recruiters

Mom, I had that nightmare again.

"The one about the actuarial recruiters who buy blood and then sell it for a higher price?"

No, that's real.

Mr. Recruiter, so you're telling me you're not actually blown away and impressed with my experience and resume...

You just... say that to everyone?

I used to reply to every recruiter with a hand-crafted, well-thought-out response with reasons why I love my current role before I realized they literally just run a query to SPAM everyone's inboxes over and over until the dawn of the apocalypse arrives.

Actuary Problem Dog
@ActuaryDog

when the recruiters email you on a friday night to congratulate you on an exam pass

robert eaton @loveactuary
Replying to @ActuaryDog
@ActuaryDog has anyone ever asked a recruiter for a portion of their recruitment fee?

Sorry babe, I wasn't listening. I thought you were an actuarial recruiter.

Recruiters be like:

- missed call work phone

- missed call cell

- voicemail

- email

- LinkedIn message

"Oh, hi just wanted to check in no big deal."

 Actuary Problem Dog
@ActuaryDog

romantic comedy: guy pretends to be an actuarial
recruiter so he can talk to this girl.. she keeps saying
"im not interested in new opportunities at this time"
but he keeps calling. she gets so frustrated that she
goes to murder him but when they meet in person she
falls in love

 Actuary? Actuarial! @actuarialtweets
Replying to @ActuaryDog
Bridget Jones's Machine Learning Diary

Retweet[44] if you drunk-email actuarial recruiters just for funsies.

Replying to actuarial recruiters and drinking Casamigos Tequila Margaritas = free therapy.

Actuary Problem Dog
@ActuaryDog

♪ on the first day of christmas a recruiter left a voicemail to tell me about the email he just sent me ♪

Daniel D Skwire @DanSkwire
Replying to @ActuaryDog
Five cellphone rings!

Matt @MLBactuary
Replying to @DanSkwire and @ActuaryDog
Four irrelevant job listings!

Nate Worrell @NateWorrell
Replying to @MLBactuary @DanSkwire and @ActuaryDog
3 referral requests

John Lee @Actuarial_Tutor
Replying to @NateWorrell @MLBactuary and 2 others
2 superfluous uses of your first name...

---

[44] A tweet is the name given to a post on Twitter. Retweeting means sharing the post with your followers. Not that actuaries have any followers, but we can dream.

If these recruiters want me to respond they're gonna have to get a LITTLE more creative than just calling my work phone, cell phone, emailing, LinkedIn messaging, cooking me dinner, showing up for family holidays, marrying into the family, etc. like c'mon show some effort!

Recruiters calling to "circle back" with you when you never even circled with them in the first place.

 Actuary Problem Dog
@ActuaryDog

would you rather:

try the tiktok pink sauce	66.7%
answer a recruiter's call	33.3% [45]

---

[45] You're clearly an actuary if you realized that the number of people who voted was a multiple of 3.

Actuary Problem Dog
@ActuaryDog

as much as I fear the blood-seeking terror of actuarial recruiters, i need to be one for a second...

i'm LOOKING FOR AN ACTUARIAL ANALYST II to join my team!

i promise it's a really fun role!

DM me if interested. must have at least a couple of exams & some actuarial experience

John Lee @Actuarial_Tutor
Replying to @ActuaryDog
Narrator: It was only "fun" in the sense that it offered distraction to actuaries from their study-filled but otherwise empty lives.

Distracted

Boss, I've been so productive today. I counted all the little square tiles on the bathroom floor.

Oh, hi boss *shuffles papers *opens Excel *spills coffee on pants[46] to look busy.

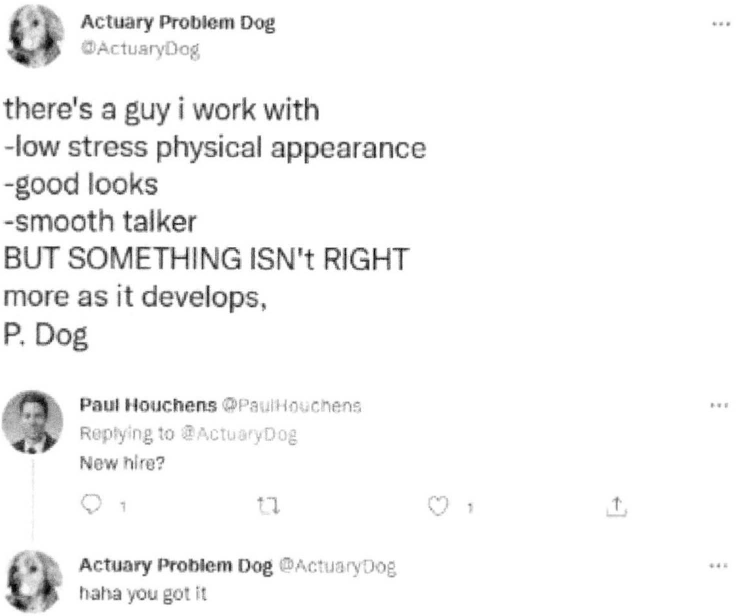
Actuary Problem Dog
@ActuaryDog

there's a guy i work with
-low stress physical appearance
-good looks
-smooth talker
BUT SOMETHING ISN't RIGHT
more as it develops,
P. Dog

Paul Houchens @PaulHouchens
Replying to @ActuaryDog
New hire?

1 1

Actuary Problem Dog @ActuaryDog
haha you got it

---

[46] I should point out to British readers, that Americans call trousers pants. He wasn't in his underwear at the office. At least we hope not. Apologies if you have now been scarred by this mental image.

Actuary Problem Dog
@ActuaryDog

he uses lots of business jargon
i'm still "reading the tea leaves" & trying to decipher it
all
let's "circle back next week"
Love,
P. Dog

> **Eliyahu Switzer** @eliyahuswitzer
> Replying to @ActuaryDog
> we need the update

Hi Team, if my Lync[47] says I'm away at any point today, it's only because I haven't moved my mouse in the last 5 mins & I might not be working.

Hi team, working from home today. I'm trying to invent caffeinated chicken soup and want to maintain an independent stream of consciousness.

---

[47] Lync was what people used before Microsoft Teams. Yes, there was a world before Teams and it was beautiful and carefree.

Disillusioned

Type in formula.

drag down

drag down

drag down

drag down

drag down

drag down

drag down

drag yourself down to the bar

have drink.

Hi Team, Taking PTO[48] today - too afraid to ask questions and have no idea what I'm doing. Call my cell. Thanks!

"Yeah, I'd be happy to share my desktop... RIGHT AFTER I CLOSE OUT MY RESUME AND COVER LETTER."

---

[48] PTO = Personal Time Out. Used by actuaries to recover from the shock of realizing that the exams have destroyed their personality.

Caught the 5:52 elevator, luckily did not have to wait for the 5:53.

"Good point, boss. I was actually thinking about that Excel workbook while I was drinking at Disney and I came up with some great ideas."

Every time I hit "Run" on a macro, I can't help but think about running away from it all.

Actuary Problem Dog
@ActuaryDog

"Where do you see yourself in 5 years?"
finally having a low-stress physical appearance but still dying on the inside

Michael Abbott @Mike_Abbott
Replying to @ActuaryDog
approximately 7.3% closer to death, depending on your choice of mortality table?

Despairing

"Hi team, working from home today. Mold in the fridge, haven't showered, lost the will to go on, etc. Call my cell if you need me, thanks."

Hey boss, is it OK if I wear sunglasses in the meeting tomorrow or is it better to let everyone see into my empty soul?

Hey, boss. Do you have time for a quick question? Should I still contribute to my 401k[49] if I don't want to live past 38?

The pumpkins, the Q4 deliverables, forgetting your coworkers' wives' names, the EXAMS. FALL[50] GLOOM is not for the faint of heart.

---

[49] American retirement savings plan. Not that actuaries ever retire.

[50] Fall is the American word for Autumn. They probably like it because it is easier to spell than Autumn.

This year's FALL GLOOM is brought to you by:

-not being able to afford any cute pumpkins

-the Roundup weed killer sitting dormant in your intestines

-the SOA still scheduling exams right after Halloween.

Existentialism

I'm not saying I believe in God, but after looking at healthcare claims every single day, I'm pretty sure Mr. God did not intend for us to live past age 39.

We're all just projections of a predetermined algorithm representing very biased views with limited data points.

Why is the accumulated value of happiness never equal to the present value of future happiness?

(Future happiness increases at lower rate).

"God, to me, isn't a man with a long white beard; he's an abstract entity who assigns the underlying probabilities for mortality rates."

Excel can exemplify the asymmetrical nature of reality by transposing artificial symmetry through a simple copy/paste special values transpose!

SOCIAL INTERACTION

Can u die from small talk?

The Art of Conversation

I'm not shy; it just takes me longer to gather data.

Trying this new thing where I smile & laugh no matter how mundane or trivial the comment is just to be fun. You guys I wanna be fun.

Actuaries are 'awkward' because being social is a weakness that causes you to fail exams. Boss, I promise I won't be social unless it's justified.

The smarter you are in math and science, the harder you are to relate to as a person.

"Hey do you have 5 minutes for a quick question?"

Actually, no. Thanks for asking! Wouldn't want to cause ripples in time and space. Have a great day!

Longest conversation I've ever had was "white, pinto, barbacoa[51], mild please, lettuce, cheese, no sour cream."

Hard to talk to someone without simultaneously giving the conversation a numerical score on a scale of 0 to 10, with 6 as passing[52].

Social tip: start talking about exams until you can think of a great question like "so what are your favorite memes?"

Actuary Problem Dog
@ActuaryDog

hope everyone is having a 6/10 day

marfle @eirsalazar
Replying to @ActuaryDog
@ActuaryDog i don't have many rational days

Avraham Adler ✓ @AvrahamAdler
Replying to @ActuaryDog
@ActuaryDog Mine is closer to
0.36363636363636363636363636363636363636363636363636363636363636
363636363636363636363636363636363636363636363636363636363636

---

[51] A Mexican food order. Probably done online to avoid having to leave the office.

[52] The American actuarial exams give students a score from 0 to 10, where 6 or higher represents a pass. Sadly normal people don't think this is important.

We go through the work day thinking of the most complex shit like all day, then someone asks "so what's new with you" and our brains suddenly stop working.

"That's why our care management program..."

Ahhh hmmmm yes yes ahhhhhhh.

Presenter: "wait what?"

Sorry. Just making listening sounds! Carry on.

I'm so bad at leaving voicemails. It's like someone took out a quarter of my brain and asked me to translate English into broken English.

Actuaries are quiet because literally all we need to feel a connection is a TI-30XS Multiview or someone standing next to us breathing.

Actuary Problem Dog
@ActuaryDog

Actuaries tweaking their personalities for the weekend

Talking-to-Listening ratio: 20%, add 1%
Overton window: Acceptable, add 5% Sensible
Alignment: True Neutral->Neutral Good
Jokes: if peer reviewed
Topics to avoid: exams, existential dread, & bitcoin

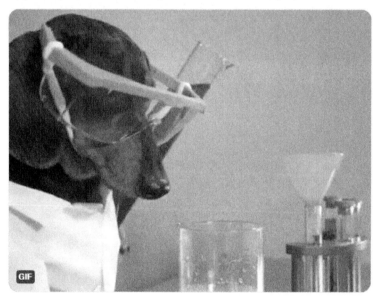

My phone just asked if it should delete all my "empty conversations." I don't mind if it reads my texts, but save the judgment.

Interacting at Work

Can't wait to go to work so I can practice making serious faces in context all day.

I don't answer the easy questions at work because I DON'T PUT OUT LIKE A SLUT - I'm only into healthy, meaningful questions with real substance.

Actuary Problem Dog
@ActuaryDog

coworkers asking detailed questions about my weekend as if our relationships are continuous and there would be no otherwise deadtime

Avraham Adler ✔ @AvrahamAdler
Replying to @ActuaryDog
@ActuaryDog be discrete. (Pun absolutely intended) 😎

I hate when my boss takes us to lunch. I work hard all day & now I have to participate in conversations about "gluten-free"?

Just wrote my co-worker a letter of recommendation for not making small talk with me this morning.

Why email your boss when you can stand awkwardly in her doorway for the most embarrassing 15 seconds of your life?

I've been having daymares about coworkers forcing me to talk about mainstream things like "the weekend" and "what I like to do for fun".

First circular reference of the day: "Hey, how's your day?" "Good, how's yours?" "Good, how's yours?" "Good, how's yours?"

"Boss, I don't know what I did this weekend because I never break character and I never think of non-work-related things while at work and I always think of work-related things while outside."

Hi team, I'm taking PTO[53] today. Call my cell if you have any questions. I won't answer but I will feel wanted and it will make my day. Thanks!

Actuary Problem Dog
@ActuaryDog

"can the external consultants also tell me how to think and feel"

Will Carbone @willcarb1
Replying to @ActuaryDog
@ActuaryDog no but we can give you a range of reasonable emotions.

What did you do this weekend? "I floated in the margins of being extroverted."

---

[53] PTO = Personal Time Out. Usually taken by actuaries who need to recover from unexpected small talk.

Actuary Problem Dog
@ActuaryDog

"the key to harnessing workflow is a sound document management" -i said that 30 times today i have no idea why

John Lee @Actuarial_Tutor
Replying to @ActuaryDog
Safer than saying "how are you?" which may involve someone talking back to you in conversation...

Last part of the day is reserved for replaying all the dumb things I said earlier & wishing I could shred the prison of my personality.

Meetings

Can we have this meeting over the phone instead? Making eye contact distracts me from listening.

People think I'm Batman because I don't announce myself on conference calls and then respond to questions in a menacing voice.

If this 40 person conference call was a party, would you stop mid-sentence to say "HI WHO JUST JOINED?" every time someone walked thru the door?

Boss, I know in the meeting I said "yeah... ummm... like... yeah..." but I promise I was thinking of like really complex shit in my head.

Still will never forgive myself for kicking off a conference call with "OK, looks like we're ready to get started! Happy Friday everyone!!!!" (It was on Good Friday)

Going out

I would go out to the bars if I could put it on my resume.

I don't think I actually know how to socialize without flirting or bringing up exams.

an actuary walks into a party

talks to no one - hovers near conversations

goes home

"Wow, I'm so exhausted."

At Great Clips, I start with $10 tip and subtract $1 for every non-hair related question, but add $5 if they already know what an actuary is.

Don't wear red to Target or someone might mistake you for an employee, a shopping cart, a wall, a cash register, a customer service desk...

 Actuary Problem Dog
@ActuaryDog

"hey wanna meet us out at the bars?"
*checks actuarial code of conduct
bars bars bars bars bars...... not seeing guidance on bars
*calls ABCD
*explains situation
(silence)
"ok yeah i think i'm allowed to partake in the barbaric pleasures of bars see you soon"

 arj @RJaliciouss
Replying to @ActuaryDog
On vacation and I almost didn't pack my calculators but I was afraid they would take away my ASA if I was caught without them

Don't let actuaries drink too much or else they'll get alcohol Poisson-ing.

Actuary Problem Dog
@ActuaryDog

eclipse OVERRATED! max 6 out of 10 experience
had more fun organizing my outlook inbox
sun and moon competing for attention/clicks - sad!

Megan Elise @MeganElise26
Replying to @ActuaryDog
But hey a 6 is still passing   54

---

[54] The American actuarial exams give students a score from 0 to 10, where 6 or higher represents a pass. Kinda similar to Meat Loaf singing "2 out of 3 ain't bad".

Small Talk

"So, what do you like to do for fun?"

Scream in my car to and from work every day.

"When someone engages in small talk with me, I do 4-digit multiplication problems in my head to keep things interesting."

"Don't trust anyone who is good at making small talk."

When people make small talk, they are literally taking cloud-based data storage in my brain (without paying for it) and forcing me to remember meaningless things (bad data) -at what point do we start charging other people for talk to us? (not soon enough)

Halloween

Worst fear: an actuarial recruiter rings my doorbell on Halloween dressed as LinkedIn and says "Resume or Treat!"

"Carving the Black-Scholes formula[55] into a pumpkin is harder than it sounds."

Last year bought 400 full-size candy bars to give out on Halloween... this year with inflation can only afford fun dip and lollipops.

Hoping the children will thank me for their lesson in market dynamics.

---

[55] A formula used to price financial options. Voted as one of the top ten formulas in the world. Yeah, actuaries are the kind of people who would rather vote on this than Love Island.

Found this in the discount section at Spirit Halloween:

Vacation

OMG! Never go to a resort! There are so many people & you might get trapped by conversation in a hot tub for an hour trying to find a way out of the conversation but your nose keeps sweating & you haven't built up enough conversational equity to exit & now you might die in the hot tub.

Thanksgiving

Boss, please don't give me Friday off. You don't know what it's like with my family.

Thanksgiving: cousin pours some non-diet coke into a plastic cup. Uncle asks about exams. Grandma has a heart attack when she hears Itô's Lemma.

Do you ever show up to other families' thanksgivings, look through the window, and just wonder what their lives are like (without exams)?

In all of the Thanksgiving dinner simulations I ran - I wind up eating all the mashed potatoes except in one extreme adverse scenario.

What kind of rice, what kind of beans, what kind of meat, what kind of salsa? IDK CHIPOTLE FOR NOW, JUST USE STANDARD ASSUMPTIONS.

Christmas

I tried explaining my job to my family and now they all think I have a learning disability.

Dear Santa, Are you a fully credentialed Santa? If not, I'm afraid I'll need your manager's signature on these "tidings of comfort and joy."

"Why expend valuable mental energy coming up with small talk topics to discuss with your extended family when you can just bring up exams?"

"Aww babe, I thought we weren't exchanging LinkedIn endorsements this year."

Social Media

Can someone please write this on my LinkedIn? "Actuary Problem Dog is on the frontier of a paradigm shift in what it means to be human."

I want to look at her LinkedIn but I don't want to give her "_____ viewed your profile" satisfaction.

"Two looks at my LinkedIn profile a day keeps the doctor away."

I used to have Facebook but someone wrote on my wall and I didn't know how to respond, so I deactivated.

Accidentally accepted a LinkedIn request within the first 5 minutes of seeing it!! I should message her to apologize & endorse her for VBA.

JUST WENT ON A WEDNESDAY NIGHT LINKEDIN RAMPAGE I EVEN ENDORSED SOME GIRL FOR "TIME MANAGEMENT".

This guy thinks I'm just going to "accept" his LinkedIn request, like I really need to increase my illusion of self-worth.

accepts request

SOMEONE KILL ME! I VIEWED HER LINKEDIN PROFILE BY ACCIDENT. NOW SHE THINKS I'M OBSESSED WITH HER, PROBABLY.

LinkedIn has been so freaking vibey lately. Even my mom is handing out endorsements like hotcakes.

~~EAT~~ STUDY ~~SLEEP~~ (PART 2)

Ask not what you can do to pass the exam
but what passing the exam can do for you

Actuarial Exams

What are "actuarial exams"???? It's when a society examines us & if our souls are empty enough they give us a numerical score of 6 or higher[56].

SOA announced all exams moving to computer-based delivery. Very exciting news for those who love the nostalgia of using Windows Vista on antiquated 2000s-era computers in Prometric[57] Centers.

MLC is like "the SI Swimsuit Edition[58] of preliminary exams".

---

[56] The American actuarial exams give students a score from 0 to 10, where 6 or higher represents a pass. Sadly passing exams doesn't correlate with success in social situations.

[57] Company that provides computerized test centers. One of the few places actuaries leave the office to visit.

[58] SI = Sports Illustrated. The annual swimsuit edition features female fashion models, celebrities and athletes wearing, unsurprisingly, swimwear in exotic locations around the world. Mostly read by young hormonal boys.

Actuary Problem Dog
@ActuaryDog

before exams..
"i want to be the first FSA that doesn't lose his soul"
after studying for 7 exams...
I DONT NEED A SOUL I HAVE GOOD JUDGMENT

Avraham Adler ✔ @AvrahamAdler
Replying to @ActuaryDog
join us in @CASact. Feel the power of the dark side. Luke, I AM your
workers comp actuary 😈

What's the point of the exams, anyway?

"I know, right? They're just a silly reflection of discipline and continued personal effort and commitment showcasing high math aptitude and problem-solving skills. Maybe I should've gotten an MBA for business acumen instead."

The exams are just a conspiracy by Big Actuary to keep us controlled so we don't CONTAMINATE the rest of the world with our affinity for misery.

Move cities, novelty wears off.

Marriage, novelty wears off.

Have kids, novelty wears off.

Pass exams, novelty was never there in first place.

So uninspiring- I heard someone say, "Everyone passes the exams eventually" AS IF WE'RE JUST PHYSICAL ALGORITHMS PASSIVELY ALONG FOR THE RIDE.

By the time we have these hoodies printed, the SOA changed the exam path again 😬

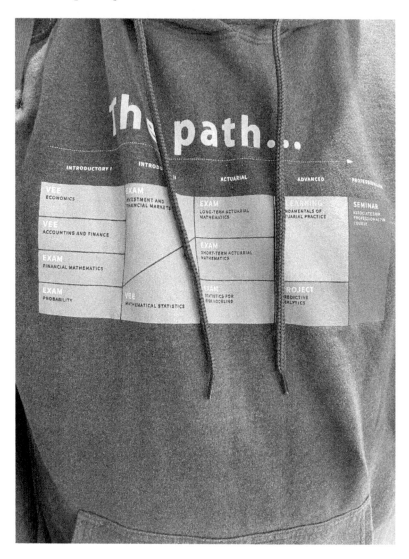

Once I get my FSA...

By the time I get my FSA I won't even want one anymore.

When the exams are finally over, maybe I'll get sad & realize life is really about the journey & exams were the best part. LOL!!!!!!!!

Tips & Tools of the Trade

Just in case the SOA goes with something other than Times New Roman, I suggest practicing exams in different fonts like Arial or Calibri.

To help prepare me for the testing environment I've been going grocery shopping during rush hour while hungry.

MLC[59] Study Tip: simulate the testing environment by not looking at your practice exam scores for 6-8 weeks.

---

[59] The results of the MLC exam take 6-8 weeks before they are released, leaving students actuaries in a state of suspended animation.

It's ~~Hammer~~ Study Time

About to start DAY ONE of studying for my last exam and I'm soooooooooo inspired thanks to the Adidas commercial I just saw.

I approach practice problems like Jeopardy[60] ... look at the answers first then ask "What is Brownian motion?"

"The exam acronyms, the calculators, the Starbucks, the Red Bull, the study manuals... they all make up a certain actuarial vernacular code."

IT'S FRIDAY NIGHT (studying, but I poured my coffee into a red solo cup[61] to create an exciting weekend atmosphere).

---

[60] An American TV quiz show where contestants are given answers and must come up with the question. Kinda like when actuaries are given an Excel file without an audit trail.

[61] Americans often drink from red plastic cups at parties. It's a form of barbarism frowned upon by the rest of the world.

I saw a vintage 2005 ACTEX FM exam manual with my bare eyes today.

Tried to stop from sneezing so I wouldn't lose precious study time but it made me sneeze harder & worser[62] & now I lost even more study time!

Actuary Problem Dog
@ActuaryDog

i just wanna do some practice problems and then have 8 or 9 drinks

Avraham Adler ✔ @AvrahamAdler
Replying to @ActuaryDog
@ActuaryDog f_drinks = drinks^(proof) / {loggamma(shot size) - drinks!}

What is exp waiting time until too tipsy to drive?

Nothing like coming home from work, cracking open a couple of beers, putting legs up on the couch, and studying for 4-6 hours.

---

[62] Yes, I know this isn't a word. It's been left in for comedic effect.

The only thing I learned from the solutions manual is that I can't trust my own thoughts.

Actuary Problem Dog
@ActuaryDog

just enough to develop an eating disorder and slowly lose sense of who I am

> **Anonymous**
> Replying to @ActuaryDog
> Out of curiosity, how many hours a day do you study?

Silly brain gets satisfied after only 4 hours of studying and persuades me to do things like "relax" or "enjoy myself".

Procrastination vs Guilt – who will win?

Maybe if I turn on the TV sports center will help me memorize this Woolhouse formula.

Currently having a dress rehearsal for my study session tomorrow: "OK, the calculator will go here and I'll procrastinate by watching YouTube."

I mean, if you're not gonna study, you might as well get blackout drunk and skip studying tomorrow too.

If you're procrastinating, make sure to stay solvent by setting up a Guilt Reserve that turns into valuable study hours once released.

"Shouldn't you be studying for MLC?" -I ask myself while showering, eating, exercising, and everything.

Pressure & perseverance

If you fail an exam three times, you lose your job or get demoted. No pressure, though!

When's your exam?

"I've been fantasizing about my own death."

OK, so 11 days?

It's hard to know what happiness feels like when you wake up in a cold sweat every morning at 6am thinking it's exam day.

4 diet cokes and 72 practice problems later, he was found breathing into a dog oxygen mask...

Actuary Problem Dog
@ActuaryDog

ExamSeasonTrendImpacts
↗ Caffeine
↗ Dread, Existential
↘ Personality (as a % of Remaining Soul)
↗ Tears PCAPM (Per Crying Actuary Per Month)

"What's up, bro? Your brain's looking jacked? How many repeats of practice problems did you do last night?"

"Well, my exam isn't until March, but I have to pull 2 all-nighters tonight to stay on pace."

Actuary Problem Dog
@ActuaryDog

i found an extra sheet of suicide note stationary if anyone needs one...

Canceling plans to study is OK. Skipping a party for studying is OK. Staying home to study is OK. Let's encourage it - Chance the Rapper, FSA.

Boss, I don't memorize, I just associate each formula with the level of anxiety I had while studying. This formula right here is 'Anxiety Lite'.

I technically make minimum wage if you factor in study time.

Big Actuary doesn't want you to see the truth behind the existential breakdowns and eating disorders that 300+ hours of studying causes.

Actuary Problem Dog
@ActuaryDog

and so it begins
officially sanctioned 12-hour study rager

Officially halfway through the #studyrager checking the scoreboard–

SOULLESS STUDYING: 6 hours

FUN: approx. 0 hours

SNACKS: 70% loss ratio

The exam

"You drank a Monster before your exam? Isn't that considered doping?"

My hand was hurting during the exam, but I was able to keep writing. #InspirationalQuote

How'd your exam go? (guide)

"I want to die" = FAILED

"Picking out my gravestone" = FAILED

*cries in public = FAILED

"Slitting my wrists" = PASSED

I'll be pretty psyched if I fail MLC because I will build so much character.

Actuary Problem Dog
@ActuaryDog

when you're taking STAM and the Prometric center only gives you two sheets of scratch paper

"Yeah, the APC is basically just Hogwarts for actuaries where you get sorted by a TI-30XS Multiview into an FSA track."

The results

Actuary Problem Dog
@ActuaryDog

by the time we get our exam results will we even care
anymore?
(about life)

Avraham Adler ✔ @AvrahamAdler
Replying to @ActuaryDog
not if you've already passed exam 3. If you're on the life side, though, you'll
always care.

Hope actuaries are prepared to be visited by the Ghost of
Exams Passed tonight.

Actuary Problem Dog
@ActuaryDog

yay! the SOA just posted solutions to the exams we all
took 101 days ago

Peter Yeates @peteryeates
Replying to @ActuaryDog
you solve them in 3 hours; they get 100 days

So many actuaries are already refreshing the SOA exam results page and it's caused Instagram to go down RIP.

"Just like a Furby[63], there's no OFF switch on the pain you feel after failing an exam."

Failing an exam is WAYY worse than getting a divorce since at least with divorce you still have half your friends and a work-life balance.

The Final Assessment is like an actuarial slumber party; except the sleeping bags are ticking time bombs and you don't get to watch movies.

Let's play Russian roulette with problems from old exams that we've passed but only faintly remember.

---

[63] A Furby was an annoying electronic talking pet that looked like a cross between an owl and a hamster. It should be noted that you can actually turn it off using a large hammer.

Starting to rethink my whole "buy a new car after each exam passed" thing.

Many students hate and reject the SOA but then pass an exam and praise the light of God... that's not God you feel bro that's the mf[64] Education Committee show some respect.

Happy FSA exam results day! May today bring you as much temporary happiness as you need in order to forget the horrors of living an introspective, analytical life.

---

[64] No, I'm not going to explain what this abbreviation stands for.

The after math

The exams taught me how to over-prepare for topics way over my head to impress others so that I can impress myself.

Studied 400 hours for MLC in May and now I can't remember a single thing I learned.

The SOA taught me how to think about worst-case scenarios. Always on my mind I can't stop, it won't stop.

Now I've qualified

 **Actuary Problem Dog**
@ActuaryDog

pouring one out to all who passed today!!!!!!
🍾🍾🍾🍾🍾
i'm finally done with exams!!

 **Eliyahu Switzer** @eliyahuswitzer
Replying to @ActuaryDog
Actuary solution dog

The long existential solitary buildup of studying for an exam was the best part of my life, and I'll never get those magical moments of self-discovery back.

"You could take the ERM exam and become a CERA."

No way man, I'm so over studying.

 Actuary Problem Dog
@ActuaryDog

i miss exams because they gave me something to blame my addictions and poor habits on, as well as an excuse to do whatever the hell i wanted whenever

now every day i stare at myself in a mirror lit by a bath&bodyworks candle and it's all an empty abyss of life and "joy"

Anonymous
Replying to @ActuaryDog
I like that name for a candle. What's the scent? Empty abyss of life and joy.

Actuary Problem Dog
@ActuaryDog

now that i am done i think they need to add two more FSA exams and increase them all to 6 hours so they can adequately test all the material

Anonymous
Replying to @ActuaryDog
A former colleague of mine described that as "climbing the tree, then pulling up the trunk after you"!

Daniel D Skwire @DanSkwire
Replying to @ActuaryDog
I heard they were adding a comprehensive oral exam to the FAC this year.

Doug Norris @NorrisDoug
Replying to @DanSkwire and @ActuaryDog
If it doesn't include flossing and mouthwash, our actuarial candidates will be at a competitive disadvantage.

Wow! None of my 79 unread emails are from actuarial recruiters! Nature is healing.

SOCIAL LIFE

Sunlight is depressing.

So much pressure to have fun!

I haven't got time...

"Yes, my calendar says I'm free from 3 to 5pm, but that's usually when I schedule my daily existential breakdown."

"My schedule is so aligned that if today's meeting runs over for even 2min it will cascade thru layers of time & I'll miss a wedding in 2032."

Of course, I have a social life...

"It's against the SOA code of professional conduct to go to bed before 10pm."

kisses my calculator goodnight

"We're going to see [a film] this weekend to fulfill our mainstream activity requirement."

I'll make up for not going out over the weekend by drinking extra Starbucks during the week.

I want to feel the pulse of the city...

Ask strangers to read an excerpt from my study materials

And feel their pulse /

//////

There's just something about frozen pizza and 33 missed calls that's synonymous with a great night out.

Vacation day? You kidding me?

I've already had lunch twice this week.

It's Saturday night. Let's listen to music and get high (-deductible health plans).

Everyone says hospitals are expensive, but there's one by me where you can get a beef wellington at the cafeteria for $4.99!

I'm going to pull 2 all-nighters tonight - not even to study just to breathe and think.

"I text my friends once every October."

No-one's habits change after age 21.

Every actuary has already found their clique and a comfortable way to complain about daily minor stresses.

The only people that call my phone are actuarial recruiters and my mom[65].

Loser of our fantasy football league has to take Exam P again and score higher than 0.

---

[65] We can infer from this statement, that Actuary Dog's mother is not an actuarial recruiter.

Of course I have a work/life balance: work > life

Going to work is a reverse opportunity cost[66] because I get less value from my social life.

Please boss, can I sleep at the office? I need to know what being sober feels like for just one night.

Yesterday metrics=17 hr work, 3 hr sleep, 2 hr misc., 1 hr coffee breaks.

Too much life this weekend - might go into the office tonight to regain work/life balance.

Why do people have pictures of their family on their desk? I have pictures of the office at home.

---

[66] Opportunity cost is the loss of other alternatives when one of them is chosen. Sadly not considered by actuaries before embarking on the actuarial exams.

Why sleep when the coffee at work is free?

I feel like Batman in Gotham city when I walk home from work at 9pm in the dark.

Then I look up at the skyline & realize I'm just an actuary[67].

"Rather work three more hours than get caught in rush hour... so he did."

Boss, please don't make me leave the office.

Please, you don't know what it's like in my apartment.

If it takes me longer than 6 minutes to fall asleep, I just go back to the office.

---

[67] Although in Batman, the villain Penguin employed an unnamed actuary to help him commit crime without getting caught. So there's certainly demand for actuaries in Gotham.

"I'm thinking you're focusing too much on work and not enough on life."

zooms in to 150% on Excel claims projection

What about now, boss?

Living on the Actuarial Edge

I've never gone white water rafting BUT I HAVE ACCIDENTALLY PASTED A 300,000 ROW EXCEL WORKBOOK INTO A WORD DOCUMENT.

I've never done drugs but once I drank a Red Bull[68] while studying.

"No grandma, I've never been lost in a corn maze, but I have worked with a file that had like 10 really weird pivot tables."

I celebrated my 21st birthday by watching an episode of Frasier and buying a life insurance policy.

---

[68] The author is referring to the energy drink and not literally putting a red bull into a blender and drinking it. He's an actuary, so lower your expectations of what exciting behavior looks like.

Forget Black Friday - I wanna blackout from drinking Monster until 4am contemplating whether it's better to be in the SOA or CAS.

I've never gone out on "wasted Wednesday" but once I copy/pasted 100,000 rows of data while a macro was running and it made me feel dizzy.

I'm going to take a shower tonight as a treat.

First Friday I've gone out in 8 months and I'm having ASM[69] separation anxiety.

---

[69] ASM (Actuary Study Materials) is a company that sells study materials for the American actuarial exams in return for the students' souls.

THE END

Almost

Review

Thank you for reading this book, or at least flipping through it until you reached this page.

As you may be aware, there are almost no actuarial comedy books on the market[70]. We could infer from this that there's simply no demand, but that would imply that us actuaries have no sense of humor.

So let's go for the alternative: it's because of a lack of awareness amongst the many fine actuaries out there which, of course, includes your good self.

Hence, to disprove the first hypothesis, we need as many people as possible to review this book on Amazon, Goodreads and elsewhere.

mybook.to/ActuaryDog

You can also tell your friends.

OK, that last one probably won't help spread the word much.

---

[70] Except, of course, the excellent *Ultimate Actuarial Joke Book* by John Lee. Not that John has edited this book and used this footnote as an opportunity for shameless promotion. Oh no.

About the author

Actuary Problem Dog is a parody Twitter account that is on the frontier of a paradigm shift in what it means to be human.

He has been tweeting his thoughts for 10 years (age last birthday) which struck a chord (or maybe a knife wound) in actuaries from around the world.

He strenuously denies the source of his humor had anything to do with being bitten by a radioactive dog.

About the editor

John was born at a very young age with his umbilical cord wrapped around his neck. At first, it appeared that no lasting damage had been done, but as he grew, it became clear that his sense of humor had been damaged irreparably.

Despite studying at Oxford University, John still refers to himself in the third person.

John trains actuaries in the UK and writes actuarial comedy books in his spare time to make up for his lack of social life.

This page has been left blank
for future funny tweets.

Although, given that the previous page has words on it, I guess it isn't really blank.

This page has also been left blank
for future funny tweets.

No pressure or anything though...

Printed in Great Britain
by Amazon

15050181R00112